Ray's Dilemma

GREGORY GRANT

Paperback: 978-1-963050-07-3
eBook: 978-1-963050-08-0
Library of Congress Control Number: 2023922482

Ordering Information:

Prime Seven Media
518 Landmann St.
Tomah City, WI 54660

Printed in the United States of America

Ray's Dilemma

Every time Ray got into trouble he ran away, until one day he could not run anymore. Ray was caught in a corner and could not get out. His aunty told him just to sit there until he had calmed down.

Ray's parents and he were involved in a nasty car accident which took both his parents and spared Ray's life. It left him scared and he began to blame himself for the accident. Ray's Aunty and Uncle took over raising him from the age of ten, but Ray became a bit of a troubled person, smoking and getting on drugs, as well as getting in trouble with the law.

His Aunty and Uncle did the best they could, but at the age of fifteen he got too hard to handle, so Ray's Aunty and Uncle decided to send him to his brother and his wife for a year, to calm down and get out of his unhealthy habits.

They rang Ray's brother and his wife to ask if they could help. They said yes. Ray's brother's name was James, and his wife was Glorify and they lived on a country property with a few cows, sheep, horses, pigs, geese, and chickens, where of course Ray would have to pull his weight.

So, the next day Ray put a few things in a bag, and they drove him to the bus to Eildon where Ray's brother lived. It took Ray an hour and half to get there. When he got there his brother James was waiting to pick him up as they lived just a couple of miles away from the bus terminal.

In about 10 minutes Ray and James were home, where Ray would live for the next year. James introduced him to another boarder by the name of Chris. Chris was in the same state of mind as Ray and there was another worker there by the name of Lee. Lee was homeless when James and Glorify found him laying in the gutter smoking and drinking when he was only thirteen.

James showed Ray around and said that he has to work if he wanted to stay there and his jobs were to milk the cows with Chris, ride to the fences and check them for damage, learn to shear the sheep with Lee, help Glorify clean up, collect eggs from the chickens and help muck out their pen. Ray said, "There is no way I will work like that." James said, "Well MATE everyone that is here must work and there is no special treatment just because you have had it hard. Just look at Lee and Chris"

So, Ray went to his room unpacked his bags and got ready for dinner. After dinner they all sat around and talked about things that happened to them and they thanked James and Glorify for taking them in. James spoke up and said, "You are all doing good work." Then they all said goodnight because they had to be up at six in the morning.

The next day was the start of the work for Ray. First, he had to help Chris to milk the cows. Ray had trouble because the cows would not stand still for him, which made him very mad and he started swearing. Chris stopped what he was doing and said, "What is wrong, "Buddy?" Ray said "The blasted cows will not stand still for me." Chris laughed and said, "Well they did that for me when I came here too. What you must do is go in front of them and tell them who is boss. They tend to listen. I know that you think that they cannot hear you, but I have worked with these cows a lot and they do get to know you."

So, Ray went in front of the cows and chatted to them, which he thought "This is stupid" but once he did, he noticed that the cows were really listening, and he could not believe what he was seeing. The cows turned to one another as if they were talking to each other. Then the main cow spoke up and said "Okkkkkkkkkkkk mooooooooo we beeeee goooooood." Ray laughed and starting milking, and each cow gave him two big buckets full of milk.

The next job he and his new-found friend Chris had to do was to ride to the fences to see if there was a damaged part. So, Ray and Chris got horses, which were named Freckles and Ride'em. Ray had Freckles and Chris had Ride'em. Ray tried and tried to get on Freckles, but Freckles was stubborn, and Chris said, "Talk to him." Ray talked to him, and said, "Be a good boy, I won't hurt you." The horse said back "Neigh I am fragile Neigh." Freckles let Ray get on him, and they both then rode down to the fence line. When they got there, they saw a few fence wires were broken, which was a job for tomorrow. Chris said that they had to get a new fence wire from the local handy mart. They rode back to tell James so he could get it tomorrow. Before the boys left the horses, they gave them some feed and water and blew them a kiss.

After Ray and Chris finished telling James about the fence, they went to wash up for lunch, which was so big and filling that Ray could not finish it all. Then he went back to work, to learn how to shear sheep with Lee. Lee told Ray: "Shearing sheep is just like having a hair cut, but you must be firm because sheep tend to play up, so you must look them straight in the eyes, and tell them who is boss. They will understand." So, before Ray started, he gave a talking-to to all the sheep and said that they needed a haircut. "Just look at your hair, it is all puffy;" The sheep said "Bah weeeeee willlll dooo ass youuu sayyy masterrr Bah."

And he started cutting being careful not to cut into them. He and Lee were amazed how the sheep just came in when you called them. They all had names, the whole 120 of them. When Ray's shearing was done, he had to sort out the wool that was worth selling from the wool that was not which they kept for insulation of the roof of the new house that James and Glorify were going to build. Then Ray swept up the bits he could not pick up.

The next thing was the chicken run where Hennie and Pennie were living in peace. James and Ray had to collect the eggs, take up the old hay which smelled, and wash the floor. After the floor was washed, they blow-dried it. When the floor was dried, they put down fresh hay which James got from the hay shed, and he spread it around making it comfortable again, with pillows on which Hennie and Pennie could lay down their feathers after an exhausting day of laying eggs and clacking around. The chickens said "Squawk, squawk, thank you squawk."

The eggs went to Glorify to cook with and for dinner they would be having an egg soufflec. By this time Ray was feeling a bit peckish but he had a few more jobs yet. He had to feed the geese and found them in the dam, swimming merrily around without a care in the world. They had to be locked up for the night, so they do not roam around. Ray said, "I could get used to this lifestyle," as he really loved the work which he was still learning.

All that Ray missed was his blue heeler 'Rusty,' but he knew that if he worked hard and did not get into any trouble and stayed off the drugs, he would get his dog, but he just wondered how Rusty was going to get down, he could not drive, Ray laughed to himself. He thought that his Aunty and Uncle will come down too. Rusty and him where close as Rusty saved Ray's life when he overdosed. Rusty was a gentle giant and would not hurt anyone unless he was threatened. Ray thought if Rusty could live with him, it would be better than the city for both. He thought "If life is this good on the farm I might live here and make new friends who are really like me in more ways than one." So, he went in then to tea and he was incredibly happy.

When tea was over Ray who was feeling tired after his exhausting day in the yard, said goodnight and went to his bedroom leaving everyone else talking for a while. The next morning, he found it hard to wake up at six, so James had to wake him. Gee was not he in a mood, wanting a smoke, but he did not have any. So, he started all his jobs again but because he was still tired, the milking of cows was challenging work today. He did one thing wrong, though, he forgot to talk to the cows, and they kicked the bucket of milk all over him. It was a funny sight and Chris stood and laughed which upset Ray even more and he refused to work until he changed his clothes, so Chris said to him to get changed.

The wire for the fence had arrived, so Chris and Ray could get on with mending the fence, but the horses were nowhere to be found. Chris called out to them "Here Freckles and Ride'em, here." But still no sight of them. They had to look for them and found them eating hay and grazing. They came over when they saw the boys. Chris got Ride'em ready and got on him, but Ray was having trouble again with Freckles. Freckles scented that Ray was not feeling the best today, so quickly Ray had to calm himself down, but it did not work. Once Ray got on Freckles, Freckles bucked and neighed and kicked like a bad little boy Ray fell off, right into a cowpat. Once again, he kicked up a stink, and went back to the house to get changed. When he came back Chris had gotten Freckles calmed down, but Freckles refused to let Ray ride him until Chris begged with Freckles and said, "If you don't ride today, you will get no feed tonight." So, Freckles said, "Ok ok neigh no need to be mean neigh. I will let the cheeky young man on." So, Ray got on and they rode down to the fence to mend the wires, which was a hard job because they had to take down the old wires and put on the new ones.

By the time they rode back it was teatime and tonight it was mud pie with greens. Ray came flying in slamming the door and glorify said, "What's wrong." Ray said, "Today has been hard and I haven't got any smokes." Chris said" If you want a smoke, I will give you one if you calm down." So, Chris and Ray went outside for a smoke and while they were out, Chris asked Ray if he was missing his Aunty and Uncle. Ray said, "Yes that I am." Chris said, "Don't worry buddy it will soon settle down." Ray said, "But I didn't get my other jobs done." Chris told him not to worry. Ray asked if he had always lived in Australia and Chris said "No. I used to live in India, but we had to leave so my foster parents could get work. When I got here, I did not get on and it became hard for my fosters." So at least Ray knew he was not the only one still thinking about his life. Then they went in to have their tea, Ray was happy, as talking to Chris calmed him down.

So, after tea they danced and drank the rest of the night away after which Ray went to bed.

The next morning Ray was the first one up, so he had to get his own breakfast which was bacon and eggs with toast. He picked up an old newspaper and read it when Lee came in looking still sleepy.

In came James who was already up and had fed the chooks. Now James did not know that Ray, Chris, and Lee could talk to the animals even though Ray was only learning, but Chris and Lee were the only ones to keep the animals under control and it was their secret-no one will ever know.

Glorify came in as chipper as ever singing to herself, so Ray asked, "Why are you so chipper?" Glorify said "It is a beautiful day today." Lee said, "I don't know about that to me it is a bum of a day." "Why is that?" asked Ray. Lee answered, "Because it is." "That's no answer," said Ray. "Well, it will have done" Lee said, "Now finish your meal." Ray finished his meal and quickly got out of there "Lee is obviously in a mood like I was yesterday." said Ray.

Lee was so unhappy he started to cry. Ray and Chris heard him crying and wondered what was wrong with him. They continued to milk the cows, but their mind was not on the job, and they missed the bucket and milk went onto the floor. They both stopped what they were doing and walked up to Lee who was not doing any work and they asked, "What's wrong Lee." Lee said, "Don't mind me, and get on with your work." But Chris and Ray asked if he wanted to talk about it. Lee opened and said, "It is the anniversary of my foster parent's death. They were shot down while just waiting to cross the road on their way to work." Chris and Ray were very comforting because they knew what it was like and they said, "Well let's do our work now and we will remember them tonight ok?" Lee said, "Thanks guys I thought you wouldn't understand." "But we do," they said, and they told the stories of their lives later that night.

And after they told Lee their stories, they all got together and said a few prayers in memory of Lee's foster parents. It was such a good night outside that they stayed out until it was bedtime and talked. They were all happy to be there laughing and chatting.

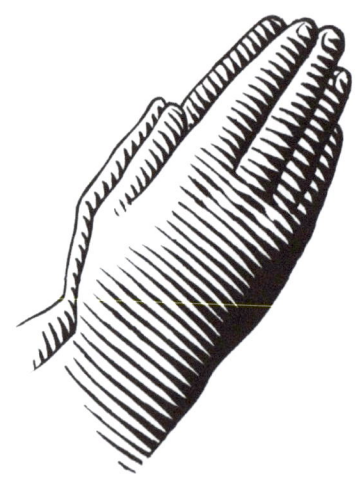

www.ingramcontent.com/pod-product-compliance
Lightning Source LLC
Chambersburg PA
CBHW041448120626
46547CB00002B/387